ARETHA FRANKLIN

by Tamika M. Murray

FOCUS
READERS®

NAVIGATOR

WWW.FOCUSREADERS.COM

Focus Readers is distributed by North Star Editions:
sales@northstareditions.com | 888-417-0195

Produced for Focus Readers by Red Line Editorial.

Content Consultant: Ronald J. Stephens, Phd, Professor of African American Studies, Purdue University

Photographs ©: Globe Photos/ZUMA Press Inc./Alamy, cover, 1; Tamika M. Murray, 2; Photofest, 4–5; AP Images, 7, 12–13; Shutterstock Images, 8–9, 10, 15, 17, 18–19, 21; NewsBase/NBBPS/AP Images, 23; Universal Pictures/Photofest, 25; Amy Sancetta/AP Images, 26–27; Red Line Editorial, 29

Library of Congress Cataloging-in-Publication Data
Names: Murray, Tamika M., author.
Title: Aretha Franklin / by Tamika M. Murray.
Description: Lake Elmo, MN : Focus Readers, 2023. | Series: Black voices on race | Includes index. | Audience: Grades 4-6
Identifiers: LCCN 2022007893 (print) | LCCN 2022007894 (ebook) | ISBN 9781637392638 (hardcover) | ISBN 9781637393154 (paperback) | ISBN 9781637394151 (pdf) | ISBN 9781637393673 (ebook)
Subjects: LCSH: Franklin, Aretha--Juvenile literature. | Soul musicians--United States--Biography. | African American singers--Biography--Juvenile literature. | Singers--United States--Biography--Juvenile literature. | Civil rights movements--United States--20th century--Juvenile literature.
Classification: LCC ML3930.F68 M87 2023 (print) | LCC ML3930.F68 (ebook) | DDC 782.421644092 [B]--dc23
LC record available at https://lccn.loc.gov/2022007893
LC ebook record available at https://lccn.loc.gov/2022007894

Printed in the United States of America
Mankato, MN
082022

ABOUT THE AUTHOR

Tamika M. Murray is an award-winning author of nonfiction books, a freelance writer, and a certified social worker. She currently resides in Southern New Jersey with her boyfriend and three rambunctious kitties.

TABLE OF CONTENTS

CHAPTER 1

RESPECT

In the song "Respect," a woman speaks to her husband. She is tired of how he treats her. She tells him to show her respect. Otherwise, she might leave him one day.

Singer Otis Redding wrote "Respect." He released his version in 1965. Aretha Franklin released a new version in 1967.

Aretha Franklin sang covers of many songs. She was known for making the songs her own.

She changed the melody. She also changed some of the lyrics. For example, she spelled out the word *respect* in the song. The song went to No. 1 on the Billboard Hot 100 music chart.

"Respect" earned Franklin her first Grammy Awards in 1968. She won for Best **R&B** Recording. She also won for Best Female R&B Solo Vocal Performance. "Respect" went on to become an **anthem**. Black people, women, and anyone feeling disrespected connected with the song.

Franklin cared about more than creating musical hits. She supported the civil rights movement, too.

Franklin shows off her Grammy Award for Best Female R&B Vocal Performance in 1975.

Franklin toured with Dr. Martin Luther King Jr. She traveled with the Reverend Jesse Jackson. She also worked with singer-**activist** Harry Belafonte. Franklin did what she could as a singer and musician to help Black people.

CHAPTER 2

GROWING PAINS

Aretha Franklin was born on March 25, 1942, in Memphis, Tennessee. She experienced great changes in her childhood. At age two, her family moved to Detroit, Michigan. At age six, her parents separated. Her mother died only four years later.

Aretha Franklin's mother, Barbara Franklin, died in 1952. This loss influenced Aretha's music. She was known for singing with great feeling.

Aretha's father, Reverend C. L. Franklin, pastored at New Bethel Baptist Church in Detroit.

Aretha found comfort in her father's church. Her father was a minister. She sang in his church choir. Aretha was a **prodigy**. She sang her first solo around age nine. She also taught herself to play the piano. At age 16, she made her first recording for Chess Records. Her father wanted her to pursue a career in music.

Aretha's father also preached about uplifting the Black race. He was friends with Dr. Martin Luther King Jr. That friendship influenced Aretha to join the civil rights movement. Music and civil rights would be lifelong passions for her.

BLACK AMERICAN CHURCHES

Being a church member is a tradition in many Black families. African Americans embraced religion during slavery. Gathering to praise God helped the enslaved people lift their spirits. But many white European American people were afraid of Black churches. They feared enslaved people were plotting against them. Even after slavery ended, some white people targeted Black churches. Yet these churches brought joy and safety to their members. Today, Black churches still represent the Black community.

CHAPTER 3

FINDING HER VOICE

Aretha Franklin moved to New York City in 1960. She signed with Columbia Records. Her early recordings included some blues and gospel songs. However, Columbia promoted Franklin as a jazz and pop singer. They insisted she use their **producers**. She had little creative say.

John Hammond signed Aretha Franklin to Columbia Records. He'd previously discovered successful musicians such as Billie Holiday.

Franklin had a few hits on the R&B and easy-listening charts. For example, "Today I Sing the Blues" was her first single for Columbia. The song made it to Billboard's R&B top 10. Her popularity grew. But Franklin did not believe Columbia could help her reach her true potential.

Franklin left Columbia Records in 1967. Then she signed with Atlantic Records. Music producer Jerry Wexler worked with her. He urged Franklin to choose her songs. It did not take long for her to succeed. She returned to singing blues and gospel songs. She soon became known as the Queen of Soul. Soul music

Franklin was with Atlantic Records for 12 years.

grew from gospel and R&B music. It is
sung with a lot of feeling. Franklin's first
album with Atlantic Records sold more
than one million copies. That album also
featured "Respect." This song quickly
became a hit.

Franklin made more albums that sold
well. And in 1971, she was the first soul

singer to play at the Filmore West. The venue was known for its rock-and-roll performers. Franklin's recorded concerts became the album *Aretha Live at Fillmore West.*

AFRICAN AMERICAN GOSPEL MUSIC

Aretha Franklin sang gospel music in her father's church choir. African American gospel music shaped her musical style. African American gospel is a form of rhythmic and spiritual music. It started from African American spirituals. Spirituals were folk songs written during slavery. Gospel music became popular during the 1930s. It led to the creation of R&B music. Gospel music continues to thrive thanks to singers like Franklin.

Franklin sang across the genres of jazz, pop, soul, and R&B. But she never left behind her roots in gospel music.

By 1972, Franklin had returned to gospel music with *Amazing Grace*. It was recorded at New Temple Missionary Baptist Church. Film director Sydney Pollack recorded Franklin's two shows. It became a **documentary**. The gospel album sold more than two million copies. It is listed in the Grammy Hall of Fame.

CHAPTER 4

THE CIVIL RIGHTS MOVEMENT

Aretha Franklin always supported civil rights. Early on, she joined her father on gospel tours. Starting at 16, she sang with Dr. Martin Luther King Jr. on the tours. In 1963, her father organized a civil rights event. It was called the Detroit Walk to Freedom. At the time, it was the largest demonstration in US history.

Dr. King's March on Washington happened two months after the Detroit Walk to Freedom. More than 200,000 people came to support civil rights.

As an adult, Franklin's quest for equality went beyond marching. She refused to sing for **segregated** crowds. That rule was written into her contracts in the 1960s. Her decision made her stand out among other singers. She also used her talent to raise money for civil rights. Franklin and singer-activist Harry Belafonte toured in 1967. The tour supported Dr. King's Southern Christian Leadership Conference (SCLC). The SCLC fought against segregation through nonviolent forms of protest.

Franklin also supported the Black Panthers. This political party fought for Black freedom. It was dedicated

Aretha Franklin was proud that her song "Respect" was linked to many social movements.

to helping Black communities. It protected Black neighborhoods from police violence. And it created the Free Breakfast for Children Program.

Franklin backed individual members of the party as well. For example, activist and professor Angela Davis was arrested in 1970. She was accused of buying weapons to help prisoners escape. Franklin offered to pay for her release from jail. Franklin said, "Angela Davis must go free. Black people will be free."[1] Later, Davis was found innocent and released.

THINK AND BE FREE

Aretha Franklin wrote the song "Think" six days after Dr. King's funeral. She wanted everyone to look at the current state of the world. She also wanted to empower people. The song gained attention because of its message. It reminded people to let themselves be free. In 1969, Franklin took her own advice. Her abusive ex-husband had been her manager. Franklin fired him. She hired her brother Cecil instead.

1. Hampton, Dream. "'Black People Will Be Free': How Aretha Lived the Promise of Detroit." NPR. Aug. 16, 2018. www.npr.org.

Franklin changed her style for *Young, Gifted and Black*. She lost her tall hairdos and wore West African pieces.

By 1972, Franklin was making music for the **Black Power** movement. She recorded the album *Young, Gifted and Black*. Franklin believed the movement encouraged Black people to look at themselves. According to Franklin, "We merely started appreciating our natural selves."[2]

2. Vincent, Rickey. *Party Music: The Inside Story of the Black Panthers' Band and How Black Power Transformed Soul Music*. Chicago: Lawrence Hill Books, 2013. p. 156.

THE BLUES BROTHERS

By 1979, disco music had become popular. People were listening less to soul music. As a result, Franklin's career stalled. So, Franklin was delighted when she was asked to act in *The Blues Brothers*. This film is a musical comedy. It is about two brothers who try to save an orphanage. They plan to reunite their old band. Then they will perform and raise money.

In the film, Franklin plays a tired waitress. Her husband had been a member of the band. The brothers want him to rejoin. But Franklin's character is not a fan of the brothers. She doesn't want her husband to rejoin. So, she sings the song "Think." The song sends a message of caution to the men. It also sends a message to all listeners.

Aretha Franklin wanted to sing "Respect" in *The Blues Brothers*. But the story relied on her singing "Think."

Lyrics about freedom echo Black Americans' continued struggle for equality. Franklin's career was reignited thanks to the film's success.

CHAPTER 5

THE GOLDEN YEARS

Aretha Franklin signed with Arista Records in 1980. She released many albums to great success. *Jump to It* sold 500,000 copies. *Who's Zoomin' Who?* sold one million copies. And *Aretha* sold 500,000 copies.

In 1987, Franklin was inducted into the Rock and Roll Hall of Fame. She was

Aretha Franklin was awarded a Kennedy Center Honor in 1994. It was only one of many achievements throughout her legendary career.

the first woman to be honored in this way. She also recorded a gospel album. *One Lord, One Faith, One Baptism* was recorded at her father's old church in Detroit.

As the years passed, Franklin continued working. In 1998, singer Lauryn Hill wrote and produced "A Rose Is Still a Rose." Franklin sang with her. The song showed that Franklin still empowered women.

Franklin's lifetime achievements were vast. She won the Presidential Medal of Freedom in 2005. The award goes to people striving to make the world more peaceful. Franklin sang during President Barack Obama's inauguration ceremony in 2009. She also earned 18 Grammy Awards during her career.

Franklin died on August 16, 2018. But her legacy lives on. In 2021, *Rolling Stone* named "Respect" the No. 1 Greatest Song of All Time. Franklin will be remembered as the Queen of Soul.

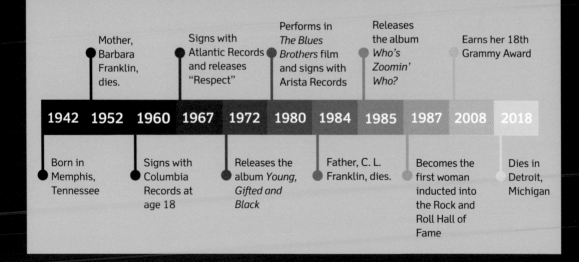

ARETHA FRANKLIN TIMELINE

1942	1952	1960	1967	1972	1980	1984	1985	1987	2008	2018

Mother, Barbara Franklin, dies.

Signs with Atlantic Records and releases "Respect"

Performs in *The Blues Brothers* film and signs with Arista Records

Releases the album *Who's Zoomin' Who?*

Earns her 18th Grammy Award

Born in Memphis, Tennessee

Signs with Columbia Records at age 18

Releases the album *Young, Gifted and Black*

Father, C. L. Franklin, dies.

Becomes the first woman inducted into the Rock and Roll Hall of Fame

Dies in Detroit, Michigan

FOCUS ON
ARETHA FRANKLIN

Write your answers on a separate piece of paper.

1. Write a paragraph that describes the main ideas of Chapter 4.

2. Do you consider Aretha Franklin an activist? Why or why not?

3. Which song was featured in *The Blues Brothers*?

    A. "Respect"
    B. "Think"
    C. "Today I Sing the Blues"

4. Why did "Respect" become so popular?

    A. It was Franklin's first rock-and-roll song.
    B. Many people could relate to the song's message.
    C. It was the first time anyone had sung about respect.

Answer key on page 32.

GLOSSARY

activist
A person who takes action to make social or political changes.

anthem
An inspiring popular song that is connected with a specific group, idea, or point of view.

Black Power
A movement that began in the 1960s and focused on Black pride and self-reliance as opposed to integration with white society.

documentary
A film or television show that presents the facts about actual events.

prodigy
A young person who is very talented.

producers
People who work with musicians to record songs.

R&B
Short for "rhythm and blues." A form of African American folk music and blues set to a strong beat.

segregated
Separate or set apart based on race, gender, or religion.

TO LEARN MORE

BOOKS

Armand, Glenda. *Black Leaders in the Civil Rights Movement: A Black History Book for Kids.* Emeryville, CA: Rockridge Press, 2021.

Elizabeth, Jordannah. *She Raised Her Voice: 50 Black Women Who Sang Their Way into Music History.* Philadelphia: Running Press Kids, 2021.

Harris, Duchess, and Tammy Gagne. *Aretha Franklin: Legendary Singer.* Minneapolis: Abdo Publishing, 2020.

NOTE TO EDUCATORS

Visit **www.focusreaders.com** to find lesson plans, activities, links, and other resources related to this title.

INDEX

Answer Key: **1.** Answers will vary; **2.** Answers will vary; **3.** B; **4.** B